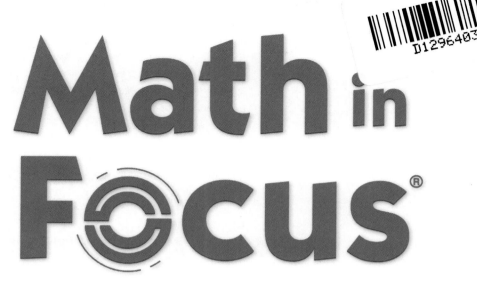

Math in Focus®

Singapore Math®
by Marshall Cavendish

Extra Practice and Homework

Program Consultant
Dr. Fong Ho Kheong

Marshall Cavendish
Education

U.S. Distributor

Houghton Mifflin Harcourt.
The Learning Company™

Course
2A

© 2020 Marshall Cavendish Education Pte Ltd

Published by Marshall Cavendish Education
Times Centre, 1 New Industrial Road, Singapore 536196
Customer Service Hotline: (65) 6213 9688
US Office Tel: (1-914) 332 8888 | Fax: (1-914) 332 8882
E-mail: cs@mceducation.com
Website: www.mceducation.com

Distributed by
Houghton Mifflin Harcourt
125 High Street
Boston, MA 02110
Tel: 617-351-5000
Website: www.hmhco.com/programs/math-in-focus

First published 2020

ISBN 978-0-358-10310-3

Printed in Singapore

3 4 5 6 7 8 9 10   1401   26 25 24 23 22
4500840182   B C D E F

The cover image shows a Eurasian lynx.
This medium-sized wild cat can be found in the thick forests of Siberia, and in remote, mountainous parts of Europe and Asia. Eurasian lynxes have dark spots on their fur, long, black tufts at the tips of their ears, and they have excellent hearing. They are nocturnal hunters that approach their unsuspecting prey very quietly from out of the darkness. Although their numbers had previously dropped due to hunting, they are now increasing once again.

Contents

Preface

Welcome!

Math in Focus® *Extra Practice and Homework* is written to complement the Student Edition in your learning journey.

The book provides carefully constructed activities and problems that parallel what you have learned in the Student Edition.

- **Activities** are designed to help you achieve proficiency in the math concepts and to develop confidence in your mathematical abilities.

- **MATH JOURNAL** is included to provide you with opportunities to reflect on the learning in the chapter.

- **PUT ON YOUR THINKING CAP!** allows you to improve your critical thinking and problem-solving skills, as well as to be challenged as you solve problems in novel ways.

You may use a calculator whenever ▦ appears.

BLANK

Name: _____ Date: _____

Chapter 1

Extra Practice and Homework
Rational Numbers

Activity 1   Representing Rational Numbers on a Number Line

Find the absolute value of each fraction. Draw a number line to show how far each fraction is from 0. Write each fraction in simplest form.

1 $\dfrac{15}{20}$

2 $\dfrac{31}{8}$

3 $-\dfrac{8}{17}$

4 $-\dfrac{30}{12}$

Write each integer or fraction as $\dfrac{m}{n}$ in simplest form, where m and n are integers.

5 5

6 -67

There may be more than one answer.

7 $-\dfrac{15}{80}$

8 $\dfrac{270}{33}$

Write each mixed number or decimal as $\frac{m}{n}$ in simplest form, where m and n are integers.

9 $2\frac{7}{12}$

10 $-1\frac{1}{21}$

11 $17\frac{2}{3}$

12 $-70\frac{5}{12}$

13 0.8

14 2.51

15 41.75

16 -0.135

17 -1.32

18 -5.52

Locate the rational numbers on each number line.

19　The thermometer below represents a number line. The readings are calibrated in degrees Celsius.
7°C, −2.5°C, −3°C, 3.5°C, −0.8°C

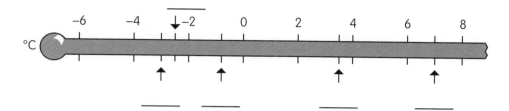

20　−2.8, 5.2, −$\frac{23}{3}$, $\frac{46}{6}$

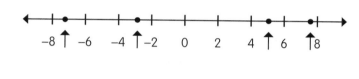

Graph each rational number on a separate number line.

21　$23\frac{2}{3}$

22　$\frac{135}{6}$

23　$-\frac{151}{21}$

24　−58.9

Refer to the list of rational numbers below for questions 25 to 32.

$$-4\frac{5}{14}, \; 6.7, \; \frac{21}{4}, \; -3.12, \; -\frac{22}{7}, \; 1.01$$

25 Order the numbers from least to greatest.

26 Write the absolute value of each number.

27 Which number has the least absolute value?

28 Compare $|-3.12|$ and $|1.01|$. Which has a greater value?

29 A and B are two numbers. Given that the absolute value of A is greater than the absolute value of B, explain whether the value of A is also greater than B.

30 Graph the numbers on a number line.

31 Which negative number in the list is farthest from 0?

32 Which number in the list is closest to −1?

Look for the two given numbers that are just on the left and just on the right of −1. Compare them and see which is closer to −1.

Chapter

1

Extra Practice and Homework
Rational Numbers

Activity 2   Writing Rational Numbers as Decimals

Using long division, write each rational number as a terminating decimal.

1 $\dfrac{7}{16}$

2 $\dfrac{51}{4}$

3 $-\dfrac{9}{24}$

4 $-3\dfrac{1}{5}$

Simplify each rational number. Then, use long division to write each rational number as a terminating decimal.

5 $\dfrac{56}{64}$

6 $\dfrac{214}{8}$

7 $-\dfrac{66}{12}$

8 $-\dfrac{126}{35}$

Using long division, write each rational number as a repeating decimal with 2 decimal places. Identify the pattern of repeating digits using bar notation.

9 $56\dfrac{5}{6}$

10 $-\dfrac{2}{11}$

Write each rational number as a repeating decimal using bar notation.

11 $\dfrac{5}{11}$

12 $-\dfrac{9}{13}$

13 $-\dfrac{246}{33}$

14 $\dfrac{199}{12}$

Refer to the list of rational numbers below for questions 15 to 17.

$$-2\dfrac{11}{17}, \ \dfrac{90}{19}, \ \dfrac{63}{10}, \ -\dfrac{171}{112}, \ 4\dfrac{13}{18}$$

15 Write each rational number as a decimal with at most 4 decimal places.

16 Using your answers in **15**, list the numbers from least to greatest using the symbol <.

17 Place each rational number on the same number line.

Chapter 1

Extra Practice and Homework
Rational Numbers

Activity 3   Adding Integers

Evaluate each sum using a number line.

1 −7 + 9

2 4 + (−7)

Use the first number as a start point on the number line.

3 8 + (−8)

4 −2 + (−5)

5 5 + (−8)

6 −10 + 10

Evaluate each sum using absolute values.

7 $18 + (-39)$

8 $62 + (-18)$

9 $-25 + 14$

10 $-43 + 72$

11 $-19 + (-32)$

12 $-57 + (-21)$

Evaluate each sum.

13 $-7 + 12 + 9$

14 $-88 + 35 + 27$

15 $14 + (-20) + (-6)$

16 $-31 + (-5) + 12$

17 −45 + (−27) + (−41)

18 16 + (−54) + 23

Solve.

19 A submarine was cruising at a depth of 340 feet below sea level. Find the depth of the submarine after it ascended 76 feet.

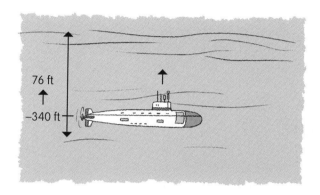

You can use the four-step problem-solving model to help you.

20 A man was standing in a valley that was 82 meters below sea level. He then climbed 726 meters to reach the summit of a nearby mountain. How high was the summit of the mountain above sea level?

21 The temperature of a substance was originally –22°C. It was left to melt and the temperature rose by 48°C. Find the final temperature of the substance.

22 Jaden draws five number cards. The number on the cards are –39, 13, –41, 28, and –17 respectively. Find the sum of the numbers on the cards.

Chapter

Extra Practice and Homework
Rational Numbers

Activity 4   Subtracting Integers

Evaluate each expression.

1 9 – 11

2 46 – 87

3 30 – 40

4 28 – (–15)

5 –14 – (–12)

6 –113 – (–58)

7 –5 – 17 – 23

8 –8 – (–12) – 31

9 –47 – (–20) – (–67)

10 –93 – (–17) – (–53)

Evaluate the distance between each pair of integers.

11 8 and 32

12 15 and 64

13 −27 and 18

14 −9 and 35

15 −24 and −11

16 −7 and −35

Solve.

17 At 2 A.M., the temperature was −6°C. An hour later, the temperature had decreased by 8°C. What was the new temperature?

18 Steven and Sarah participated in a gaming competition. Steven's final score was 480 points. Sarah's final score was 570 points less than Steven's final score. What was Sarah's final score?

19 A diver was swimming at a depth of 28 feet below sea level. He then dove 35 feet further. What was his new depth below sea level?

20 The largest recorded temperature change over a 24-hour period occurred on January 15, 1972 in Loma, Montana in the United States. The temperature increased from −54°F to 49°F. Find the temperature change.

21 The highest elevation of the continent of North America is at Mt. McKinley, which is 20,320 feet above sea level. The lowest elevation is at Death Valley, which is 282 feet below sea level. What is the difference in the elevations of the two locations?

4 Subtracting Integers

22 The highest temperature ever recorded on Earth was 134°F at Death Valley, California, in 1913. The lowest temperature ever recorded was −129°F at Vostok Station, Antarctica in 1983. Calculate the difference between these temperatures.

23 The lowest recorded temperature in Oklahoma is −31°F. The lowest recorded temperature in South Dakota is 27°F lower than the lowest recorded temperature in Oklahoma. What is the lowest recorded temperature in South Dakota?

24 The table shows the points Luis, Jada, and Matthew scored in a computer game.

Name	Game Point
Luis	−65
Jada	−84
Matthew	−73

Which two children have the closest points? Explain.

Chapter 1

Extra Practice and Homework
Rational Numbers

Activity 5   Multiplying and Dividing Integers

Evaluate each product.

1 $7 \cdot (-9)$

2 $12 \cdot (-8)$

3 $-3 \cdot 11$

4 $-5 \cdot 6$

5 $-6 \cdot (-8)$

6 $-7 \cdot (-15)$

7 $-30 \cdot (0)$

8 $0 \cdot (-19)$

9 $4 \cdot (-6) \cdot (10)$

10 $7 \cdot 8 \cdot (-9)$

Evaluate each product.

11. $-11(5)(-4)$

12. $-2(-21)(3)$

13. $6(-14)(-7)$

14. $-4(-28)(-9)$

15. $-3(-12)(-10)$

16. $-8(0)(-27)$

17. $-50(-6)(0)$

18. $-9(-8)(2)(3)$

19. $-5(7)(-4)(-5)$

20. $-10(-3)(-6)(-2)$

Evaluate each quotient.

21 $357 \div (-7)$

22 $560 \div (-16)$

23 $-720 \div 12$

24 $-550 \div 11$

25 $-189 \div (-9)$

26 $-112 \div (-4)$

27 $0 \div (-20)$

28 $0 \div (-5)$

Solve.

29 A hot air balloon descended 3,240 feet in an hour. Find the change in altitude per minute.

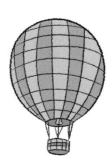

30 A diver descends at a rate of 4 feet per minute. How far is the diver below sea level after 20 minutes?

31 The average change in a company's sales income was $9 million over 3 months. Determine the average change in sales income per month.

32 A company lost an average of $30,000 per month. Find the total loss of the company in 1 year.

Extra Practice and Homework
Rational Numbers

Activity 6   Order of Operations with Integers

Evaluate each expression.

1 $-5 \cdot 8 + 12$

2 $3 \cdot (-9) + (-2) \cdot (7)$

3 $-35 - 490 \div 7 + 12$

4 $82 - (9 - 13) \cdot 9$

5 $-27 - (4 + 4) \cdot 3$

6 $90 \div (-6 - 3) + 45$

7 $-30 + 5(3 + 8) - 45$

8 $25 \div [-4 + (-1)] - 9(3)$

9 $36 \div 6 - (-25 + 15)(4)$

10 $-200 + 32(-3 + 7) - 45(15 - 20)$

Solve.

11 Callia has an 8-inch by 12-inch sheet of rectangular paper. She cuts out identical 4-inch by 3-inch rectangles from all four corners of the paper. Using the diagram shown, find the area of the remaining paper.

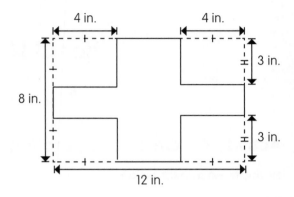

12 A water tank contained 10,000 gallons of water at first. Every week, 300 gallons of water were pumped out of the tank while 250 gallons of water were pumped back into it. Find the volume of water in the water tank at the end of 20 weeks.

Form an expression to represent the situation. Then, evaluate it using the rules of the order of operations.

Chapter

Extra Practice and Homework
Rational Numbers

Activity 7   Operations with Fractions and Mixed Numbers

Evaluate each expression. Give your answer in simplest form.

1 $-\dfrac{8}{3} + \dfrac{1}{4}$

2 $\dfrac{4}{15} + \left(-\dfrac{7}{9}\right)$

3 $\dfrac{1}{6} - \left(\dfrac{-2}{3}\right)$

4 $-\dfrac{1}{5} - \dfrac{2}{15}$

5 $\dfrac{1}{3} - \left(-\dfrac{2}{5}\right) - \dfrac{3}{4}$

6 $\dfrac{-4}{9} + \left(\dfrac{-5}{6}\right) + \left(\dfrac{-1}{3}\right)$

Evaluate each product. Give your answer in simplest form.

7 $-\dfrac{3}{4} \cdot \dfrac{5}{12}$

8 $-2\dfrac{1}{4} \cdot \dfrac{8}{27}$

9 $-\dfrac{14}{25} \cdot \left(-1\dfrac{3}{7}\right)$

10 $1\dfrac{8}{27} \cdot \left(-2\dfrac{2}{5}\right)$

11 $-2\frac{2}{3} \cdot \left(-3\frac{3}{4}\right)$

12 $\frac{2}{15} \cdot \left(-1\frac{2}{3}\right)$

Evaluate each quotient. Give your answer in simplest form.

13 $-\frac{1}{4} \div \frac{3}{8}$

14 $\frac{2}{5} \div \left(-\frac{4}{35}\right)$

15 $1\frac{2}{3} \div \left(-3\frac{1}{3}\right)$

16 $-2\frac{3}{4} \div \left(-1\frac{3}{8}\right)$

17 $\dfrac{-10}{\left(\frac{5}{13}\right)}$

18 $\dfrac{\left(\frac{2}{3}\right)}{-16}$

19 $\dfrac{\left(-\frac{4}{5}\right)}{\left(-\frac{7}{20}\right)}$

20 $\dfrac{\left(-2\frac{2}{5}\right)}{\left(1\frac{1}{5}\right)}$

Solve.

21 A restaurant used $8\frac{5}{6}$ pounds of rice on Monday, and $5\frac{1}{6}$ pounds of rice on Tuesday. How many more pounds of rice were used on Monday than on Tuesday?

22 Riley has $9\frac{2}{3}$ feet of cloth. She needs to cut it into lengths of $\frac{1}{3}$ foot. How many complete lengths can she cut?

23 A recipe calls for $2\frac{1}{2}$ cups of walnuts. A chef has only $\frac{5}{6}$ cup of walnuts. How many more cups of walnuts does the chef need for the recipe?

24 The sum of two mixed numbers is $-9\frac{2}{3}$. One of the numbers is $-2\frac{7}{9}$. Find the other number.

25 The masses of Parcel P, Parcel Q, and Parcel R are $4\frac{1}{2}$, $3\frac{2}{5}$, and $6\frac{4}{5}$ pounds respectively. Find the average mass of the three parcels.

26 A mixed number is divided by $1\frac{4}{5}$, and the quotient is $2\frac{1}{3}$. What is the mixed number?

Extra Practice and Homework
Rational Numbers

Activity 8   Operations with Decimals

Evaluate each sum or difference.

1 −3.15 + 7.9

2 0.072 + (−5.3)

3 −41.36 + (−8.2)

4 8.22 − (−0.355)

5 −17.203 − 0.86

6 −29.5 − (−9.34)

Evaluate each product.

7 0.4 · (−5.7)

8 −2.7 · 3.1

9 −4.36 · (−1.8)

10 3.04 · (−6.3)

Evaluate each quotient.

11 $-36.9 \div 4.5$

12 $159.12 \div (-3.4)$

13 $-49.14 \div (-6.3)$

14 $12.376 \div 0.52$

Evaluate each expression.

15 $-0.48 + (-0.1) + (-2.3)$

16 $-3.59 + 16.7 + (-150.06)$

17 $49.03 + (-7.8) - (-21.05)$

18 $601.03 - 467.9 + (-8.12)$

19 $21.4 - 6.2 + 4.2 \cdot 0.3 - 2.6$

20 $(39.3 + 6) \div 3 + 0.8 \cdot 4$

Solve.

21 On Sunday, the balance in Ms. Anderson's savings account was $315.12. On Monday, she made withdrawals of $78.95 and $143.80. On Tuesday, she made a deposit of $63.79. What was the balance in her savings account after she made the deposit?

22 The table shows the transactions in Mr. Johnson's savings account.

Date	Deposit	Withdrawal	Balance
January 31	–	–	$148.20
February 5	$35.65	$182.30	$1.55
February 18	$120.83	$78.32	?

What was the balance in Mr. Johnson's savings account on February 18?

23 The surrounding temperature of a town rises by 0.9°C per hour for 2 hours. It then rises by 1.2°C per hour for 3 hours. Find the total change in temperature.

24 In 2016, a company reported a net income loss of $23,800,000. In 2017, the company reported a net income gain of $10,400,000. In 2018, the company reported an earning of $800,000 more than in 2017. How much more did the company earn in 2018 than in 2016?

25 Lauren has only $10 to pay the cost for three art projects. The cost of the projects are $2.50, $6.75, and $2.80. How much more does she need?

© 2020 Marshall Cavendish Education Pte Ltd

26 The average temperature in January is −9.7°F in Fairbanks, Alaska. The average temperature in May is 49.5°F. The average temperature in September is 4.1°F less than the average temperature in May. On average, how many degrees colder is Fairbanks in January than in September?

27 A ball was rolled along a straight path. It moved at a speed of 0.6 meters per second for 8 seconds before it hit the wall and bounced back at a speed of 0.4 meters per second. Given that the ball stopped 4 seconds after it hit the wall, find the distance where the ball stopped from its starting point.

28 Mr. Clark deposits $4,300 in a savings account. The bank will pay him 4% interest at the end of a year. How much will he have in his savings account after 1 year?

29 The table shows the temperatures for the first 5 days of January in Lansing, Michigan. Find the average temperature for these 5 days.

January	1	2	3	4	5
Temperature (°C)	−5.2	−6.7	−9.1	−10.3	−8.6

30 Ms. Nelson has $50. She wants to buy a book that costs $26.50 and a bag that costs $19.50. The sales tax in her state is 6%. Does Ms. Nelson have enough money to buy the book and the bag? If so, how much does she have left? If not, how much more does she need?

1 **Mathematical Habit** **3** **Construct viable arguments**

Joshua and Jordan looked at the mathematical statement below and each arrived at their conclusion.

$$3 + (7 \times 8) - 10$$

Joshua said the brackets were not needed but Jordan said otherwise. Who is correct? Explain.

PUT ON YOUR THINKING CAP!

1 **Mathematical Habit 7** Make use of structure

If you start with an integer, and subtract −85, add −57, subtract 68, add −77, add 55, and subtract −73, the result is 0. Find the integer that you start with.

2 **Mathematical Habit 7** Make use of structure

For each of the following equations, insert brackets so that each equation is a true statement.

a $-20 + 4 \cdot 2 + 7 - 35 = -19$

b $-15 - 30 \div 10 - 15 = -9$

c $-(-5) + 4 \cdot 2 - 7 = -45$

d $9 - 15 \cdot 2 - 4 = 12$

3 **Mathematical Habit 8** Look for patterns

A multiplication magic square is a square in which the product of the numbers in each horizontal, vertical, and diagonal line is a constant. Complete the magic square by finding the missing numbers.

−24	36	2
1		144
	4	

© 2020 Marshall Cavendish Education Pte Ltd

32 **Chapter 1** Rational Numbers **Extra Practice and Homework** Course 2A

Chapter 2

Extra Practice and Homework
Algebraic Expressions

Activity 1   Adding Algebraic Terms

Simplify each expression.

1 $7x + (-9x)$

2 $-2y + 7y$

3 $17p + (-8p)$

4 $-27q + (-14q)$

Simplify each expression with decimal coefficients.

5 $0.8x + 0.5x$

6 $0.1y + 0.9y$

7 $0.8m + 2.7m$

8 $1.1b + 2.8b$

9 $1.4p + (-0.3p)$

10 $-2.3a + 0.8a$

Simplify each expression with fractional coefficients.

(11) $\frac{1}{7}p + \frac{5}{7}p$

(12) $\frac{3}{5}a + \frac{2}{5}a$

(13) $\frac{4}{9}m + \left(-\frac{2}{9}m\right)$

(14) $-\frac{5}{8}b + \frac{1}{8}b$

Simplify each expression with fractional coefficients by rewriting the fractions.

(15) $\frac{4}{7}x + \frac{5}{14}x$

(16) $\frac{2}{5}y + \frac{3}{10}y$

(17) $\frac{3}{8}p + \frac{3}{16}p$

(18) $\frac{2}{9}m + \frac{2}{3}m$

(19) $\frac{2}{3}x + \left(-\frac{1}{4}x\right)$

(20) $-\frac{5}{12}y + \frac{3}{4}y$

Solve.

21 The figure shows triangles A and B. Write and simplify an algebraic expression for the sum of the perimeters of the two triangles.

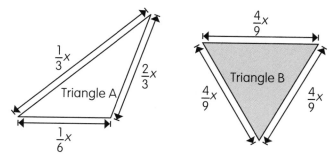

22 The length and width of two rectangular greetings cards are as shown. Find the sum of the areas of the two cards.

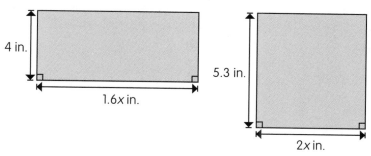

23 The number of adults to the number of children in a movie theater is 7 : 4. There are m children in the theater. Write an algebraic expression for the number of adults in the theater.

24 Hailey had q pears and some oranges. The number of oranges she had was $\frac{5}{8}$ times the number of pears she had. She then bought another 11 oranges. Write an algebraic expression for the number of oranges she had in the end.

Chapter 2 Extra Practice and Homework
Algebraic Expressions

Activity 2 Subtracting Algebraic Terms

Simplify each expression.

1 $-23x - 9x$

2 $18y - (-8y)$

3 $-36a - (-19a)$

4 $-57b - 39b$

Simplify each expression with decimal coefficients.

5 $1.7x - 0.5x$

6 $1.9y - 1.6y$

7 $2.4p - (-1.8p)$

8 $3.2a - (-2.9a)$

9 $-3.8q - 2.5q$

10 $-1.3b - 0.9b$

Simplify each expression with fractional coefficients.

11 $\frac{7}{9}x - \frac{4}{9}x$

12 $\frac{6}{7}y - \left(-\frac{2}{7}y\right)$

13 $-\frac{9}{10}p - \frac{7}{10}p$

14 $-\frac{5}{8}m - \left(-\frac{3}{8}m\right)$

Simplify each expression with fractional coefficients by rewriting the fractions.

15 $\frac{4}{5}y - \frac{1}{3}y$

16 $\frac{5}{6}x - \frac{4}{5}x$

17 $\frac{7}{9}p - \left(-\frac{1}{3}p\right)$

18 $\frac{10}{3}m - \left(-\frac{7}{4}m\right)$

19 $-\frac{9}{7}a - \frac{1}{3}a$

20 $-\frac{7}{10}b - \frac{2}{5}b$

Solve.

21 The length of Rope A and Rope B are shown. Find the difference in the length of the two ropes.

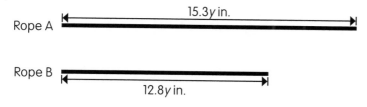

Rope A |← ——————— 15.3*y* in. ——————— →|

Rope B |← ——— 12.8*y* in. ——— →|

22 The mass of a spoon is *c* kilograms. The mass of a cup is 2.5 times the mass of the spoon. Write an algebraic expression for the difference between the mass of the spoon and the mass of the cup.

23 The length and width of a rectangular photo frame with a shaded border are as shown. Find the area of the shaded border.

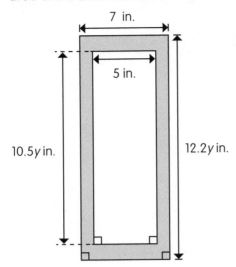

7 in.

5 in.

10.5*y* in.

12.2*y* in.

Chapter 2

Extra Practice and Homework
Algebraic Expressions

Activity 3 Simplifying Algebraic Expressions

Simplify each expression with one variable.

1 $2.1x + 0.8x - 3$

2 $1.6y + 1.9y + 1.3$

Group the like terms together.

3 $3.5p + (-2.8p) - 1$

4 $\frac{5}{9}a + \frac{4}{9}a + \frac{5}{9}$

5 $\frac{7}{8}b + \frac{1}{4}b - 3$

6 $\frac{9}{2}m + \left(-\frac{1}{3}m\right) + 7$

Simplify each expression with three algebraic terms.

7 $1.5x + 0.8x + 0.6x$

8 $5.4a - 2.7a + (-0.8a)$

9 $4.8b + 1.2b - 3.9b$

10 $\frac{1}{7}p + \frac{4}{7}p + \frac{1}{7}p$

11 $\frac{7}{9}q + \frac{1}{3}q + \frac{1}{9}q$

12 $\frac{3}{4}m + \frac{2}{3}m + \left(-\frac{1}{6}m\right)$

Simplify each expression with one variable.

13 $7a - 5 - 3a$

14 $16b - 9 + 5b$

15 $1.1p + 2.3 + (-0.5p)$

16 $6.3q - 1.8 - 5.7q$

17 $\frac{3}{5}m + \frac{2}{3} + \frac{7}{10}m$

18 $\frac{5}{6}n - \frac{2}{3} + \left(-\frac{1}{2}n\right)$

Simplify each expression with two variables.

19 $5x + x + 5y$

20 $24m - 16m - (-5n)$

21 $11a + 3a + 5b - b$

22 $9b - 2a + 3b + (-a)$

23 $2.7m + 0.5m + 3.2n + 0.8n$

24 $18.5p - 16.6p - 4.3q - (-2.7q)$

25 $\frac{3}{7}x + \frac{1}{7}x - \frac{1}{6}y + \frac{5}{6}y$

26 $\frac{3}{4}p + \left(-\frac{1}{2}p\right) + \frac{5}{9}q - \frac{1}{3}q$

3 Simplifying Algebraic Expressions

Find the perimeter of each figure.

27

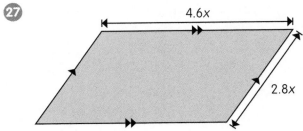

28

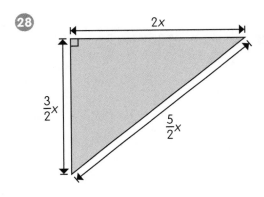

Chapter 2

Extra Practice and Homework
Algebraic Expressions

Activity 4   Expanding Algebraic Expressions

Expand each expression.

1 $\frac{1}{4}(8x + 16)$

2 $\frac{1}{3}(3p + 12)$

3 $\frac{1}{2}(14k - 10)$

4 $\frac{1}{8}(8a - 24)$

5 $\frac{1}{2}(4p + 1)$

6 $\frac{1}{7}(2a + 5)$

7 $\frac{1}{5}(3b - 2)$

8 $\frac{3}{5}(2k - 15)$

9 $2(6x + 0.1)$

10 $5(0.3y + 2)$

11 $0.3(5x + 3)$

12 $0.4(2h + 7)$

13 $0.6(m - 4)$

14 $0.5(p - 3)$

15 $0.2(1.2d + 0.3)$

16 $1.5(0.4x - 1.3)$

Expand each expression with a negative factor.

17 $-3(x + 2)$

18 $-5(2x + 3)$

19 $-2(3a + 7b)$

20 $-7(4k - h)$

Use the distributive property to multiply the negative factor.

21 $-6\left(\dfrac{1}{2}p + 3\right)$

22 $-\dfrac{1}{4}\left(8x - \dfrac{1}{3}\right)$

23 $-3(4k + 1.2)$

24 $-4(0.3m + 7)$

25 $-5(q - 0.6)$

26 $-0.2(0.6y - 2)$

Expand and simplify each expression.

27 $2(3y + 2) + 5$

28 $4(3a + 1) - 2$

29 $3(x + 8) + 5x$

30 $7(b + 4) - 3b$

4 Expanding Algebraic Expressions

31 $3\left(\dfrac{1}{4}a + 2\right) + 5$

32 $6\left(\dfrac{1}{12}a - 3\right) - \dfrac{1}{2}a$

33 $0.4(x + 3) + 0.8x$

34 $0.3(y + 5) - 0.1y$

35 $-3(5m + 1) - m$

36 $12 - 4(n - 2)$

37 $-0.6(r + 4) + 2.5r$

38 $-(1.4x + 5) + 1.7x$

Expand and simplify each expression with two variables.

39 $15y + 4(8y + x)$

40 $9a + 7(2a - b)$

41 $6g + 8(v - g)$

42 $12p + 10(p - 2q)$

43 $7(2a + b) + 2(3a + b)$

44 $4(2m - n) + 8(3n - m)$

45 $5(3d + e) - 4(d - 4e)$

46 $6(4q - p) - (2q - 5p)$

47 $-3(x + 2y) + 4(3x - 6y)$

48 $-8(y + 3t) - 4(2y - t)$

4 Expanding Algebraic Expressions

Write an expression for the missing dimension of each shaded figure and a multiplication expression for its area. Then, expand and simplify the multiplication expression.

49

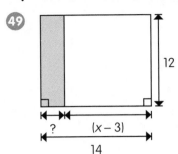

50

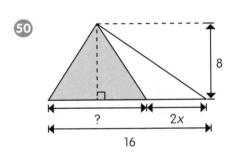

Write an expression for the area of the figure. Expand and simplify.

51

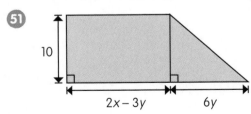

Chapter 2

Extra Practice and Homework
Algebraic Expressions

Activity 5 Factoring Algebraic Expressions

Factor each expression with two terms.

1. $8a + 8$

2. $4x - 28$

3. $6a + 6b$

4. $21p + 7q$

5. $16w + 80m$

6. $3j - 18k$

7. $12t - 48u$

8. $25a - 5p$

9. $16x - 10y$

10. $24a - 6b$

Factor each expression with negative terms.

11   $-3 - p$

12   $-y - 8$

13   $-2a - 4$

14   $-3x - 24$

15   $-7k - 35$

16   $-9u - 81$

17   $-24x - 18y$

18   $-35m - 20n$

19   $-28w - 7q$

20   $-48y - 16x$

Factor each expression with three terms.

21 $3x + 3y + 9$

22 $4a + 2b + 6$

23 $15p + 5q + 10$

24 $18d + 9e + 12$

25 $4s - 8t - 20$

26 $7a - 14b - 28$

27 $16a - 12b - 6$

28 $33g - 11h - 66$

Solve.

29 A triangle has an area of $(16p + 56q)$ square units. Its base is 8 units. Factor the expression for the area to find an expression for the height of the triangle.

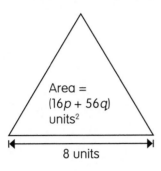

Area =
$(16p + 56q)$
units^2

8 units

30 A cuboid with square base has a volume of $(147p - 245q)$ cubic centimeters. The length of the square base is 7 centimeters. Find an expression for the height of the cuboid.

? cm

7 cm

Chapter 2

Extra Practice and Homework
Algebraic Expressions

Activity 6   Writing Algebraic Expressions

Translate each verbal description into an algebraic expression. Simplify the expression when you can.

1 Sum of one-half t and one-third s

2 Twenty subtracted from $\frac{15}{23}b$

3 Product of $5r$ and 7 divided by 15

4 120% of the sum of w and one-twelfth u

5 Nine-fourteenths of $6x$ reduced by 10

6 20% of one-half w

7 Seven-tenths of the product of $5p$ and 3

8 Sum of x, three-fourths x, and 90% of z

9 Four times the difference of one-half x subtracted from three-eighths y

10 60% of the difference of five-eighteenths v subtracted from four-sixths w

Solve. You may use a diagram, model, or table.

11 The length of a picture frame is $(8u - 12)$ inches. Its width is $\frac{3}{4}$ of its length. Express the width of the picture frame in terms of u.

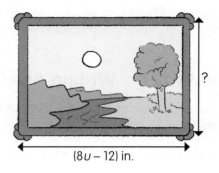

$(8u - 12)$ in.

12 6 tablespoons are equivalent to 1 fluid ounce. How many fluid ounces are in $(10t - 4)$ tablespoons?

13 11 notebooks were added to w notebooks. 7 friends then shared the notebooks equally. Express the number of notebooks each person received in terms of w.

14 A pear costs $0.40 and an apple costs $0.25. What is the total cost of
p pears and 9 apples?

15 The ratio of the number of pencils to pens is 5 : 7. There are *q* pens. Express
the number of pencils in terms of *q*.

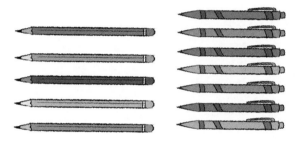

16 When 5 adults joined a group of *y* diners, the ratio of the number of adults
to children in the restaurant became 3 : 5. Express the number of children in
terms of *y*.

17 Mr. Garcia paid *w* dollars for a camera and $120 for an additional camera lens. How much did Mr. Garcia pay for the camera and lens, including a 8% sales tax?

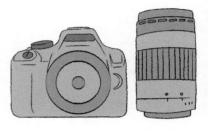

18 Emma has $5u$ game cards. Jesse has $\frac{8}{13}$ fewer game cards than Emma. Find the average number of game cards that Emma and Jesse have in all in terms of u.

19 A train traveled at 140 miles per hour for $2\frac{1}{14}x$ hours, and $(2x - 3)$ miles per hour for the next 3 hours.

a Express the total distance traveled by the train in terms of x.

b What is the total distance traveled by the train when $x = 3$?

Chapter 2

Extra Practice and Homework
Algebraic Expressions

Activity 7 Real-World Problems: Algebraic Reasoning

Solve each question using algebraic reasoning.

1. Michael has two ropes. The longer rope is $(12.5x + 17)$ centimeters long, and the shorter rope is $(5x + 0.4w)$ centimeters long. Find the difference in length of the two ropes.

2. A printing machine prints $(8w + 22)$ books in 20 minutes. Find the average number of books the machine prints in 1 minute.

3 The average daily sales at a bookstore was $(7.6k + 2.2)$ dollars over a 4-day promotion. Find the total sales during the promotion.

4 The ratio of the number of red balloons to yellow balloons is 17 : 6. The number of red balloons is $2m + 5$. How many yellow balloons are there?

5 During summer vacation, 36% of c children went to Europe, 24 children stayed within the US, and the rest of the children went to South America. How many children went to South America?

6 The hourly rates for a parking garage are as follows:

First hour	$4.00
Each additional hour thereafter	$3.20

Gabriella parked her car in the garage for y hours. How much was her parking fee?

7 A cylinder contains $(4.5x + 2y - 6)$ milliliters of liquid. How many milliliters of liquid must be added to the cylinder to make a total of $(6.9x - 3y + 3)$ milliliters?

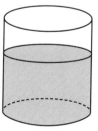

$(4.5x + 2y - 6)$ mL

8 Among the 50 children at a book fair, b of them are boys. 30% of the girls at the book fair are younger than twelve years old while 40% of the boys are at least twelve years old. How many children at the book fair are younger than twelve years old?

9 When $\frac{2}{3}b$ guppies were given away, there were still b guppies and k goldfish left in a fish bowl. How many guppies and goldfish were there initially?

10 The ratio of the mass of Bottle A to Bottle B to Bottle C is 7 : 5 : 11. The total mass of Bottle A and Bottle C is $(2x - 9)$ kilograms.

a Express the mass of Bottle B in terms of x.

b Find the mass of Bottle B when $x = 15$.

Mathematical Habit **3** **Construct viable arguments**

The following shows Cole's working.

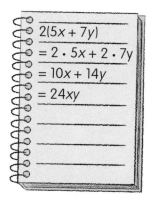

2(5x + 7y)

= 2 · 5x + 2 · 7y

= 10x + 14y

= 24xy

Is Cole's working correct? Explain.

1 | Mathematical Habit **7** Make use of structure

Brandon is thinking of three numbers. The first number is 3 less than $\frac{8}{5}$ of the second number, and the second number is $\frac{5}{16}$ of the third number. The third number is $\frac{2}{3}x - 12$. Express the first number in terms of x.

2 | Mathematical Habit **7** Make use of structure

$\frac{3}{7}$ of Jar A is filled with water. The capacity of Jar B is p pints. When all the water from Jar A is poured into Jar B, it only fills 8 pints more than 30% of Jar B. When the water is poured into Jar C, it fills 5 pints less than half the capacity of Jar C.

a What is the capacity of Jar A in terms of p?

b What is the capacity of Jar C in terms of p?

Chapter 3
Extra Practice and Homework
Algebraic Equations and Inequalities

Activity 1 Identifying Equivalent Equations

Determine whether each pair of equations are equivalent. Explain your answer.

1 $4x + 1 = 9$ and $2x + 1 = 5$

2 $y + 5 = 7$ and $5y = 10$

3 $5z - 3 = 4$ and $z = -1$

4 $7m + 6 - 5 = 15$ and $2m + 5 = 9$

5 $\frac{2}{5}x - 3 = 1$ and $\frac{3}{4}x = \frac{15}{2}$

6 $-3x + 4 = 1$ and $x = -1$

The equations are equivalent if they have the same solution.

Match each equation with an equivalent equation.

7 $8x = 16$

a $x = 1$

8 $x + 3 = 6$

b $x = 2$

9 $2x + 13 = 9$

c $2x = 6$

10 $4 - 5x = -1$

d $3x - 4 = 14$

11 $\frac{1}{3}x - 2 = 0$

e $1 + x = -1$

Extra Practice and Homework
Algebraic Equations and Inequalities

Activity 2   Solving Algebraic Equations

Solve each equation with variables on the same side.

1 $5x + 3 = 7$

2 $4y - 7 = 5$

3 $9p + 5 = -13$

4 $23 = 6x - 1$

5 $\frac{2}{3}x - 5 = 1$

6 $\frac{7}{5}y = 3 - \frac{1}{5}$

7 $\dfrac{5}{8}p = \dfrac{9}{4} - \dfrac{3}{8}$

8 $\dfrac{5}{6} = \dfrac{3}{4}x - \dfrac{2}{3}$

9 $5.7 + 0.3y = 6.9$

10 $4.2 + 2.5a = 9.2$

11 $3.2y - 7 = 9$

12 $7.8y - 4.9 - 5.4y = 2.3$

Solve each equation involving parentheses.

13 $4(3x - 2) = 16$

14 $5(4y - 3) = 45$

15 $3(4n - 1) - 7n = 17$

16 $6(5c - 2) - 10c = 13$

17 $\frac{3}{4}(5a - 3) = \frac{3}{8}$

18 $\frac{4}{5}(m - 1) - \frac{1}{5}m = 1$

Work out the expressions in the parentheses first.

19 $\dfrac{2}{5}x - \dfrac{1}{4}(x - 8) = \dfrac{13}{2}$

20 $6(3.2y - 1) = 3.6$

21 $1.8(5a + 3) + 5.6 = 29$

22 $\dfrac{6}{5}(2f - 3) - 3f = \dfrac{3}{2}$

23 $0.5(2m - 3) - 0.8m = 2.7$

24 $0.8(3.5h - 5) = 1.6$

Chapter 3

Extra Practice and Homework
Algebraic Equations and Inequalities

Activity 3   Real-World Problems: Algebraic Equations

Solve.

1 Ms. White had x dollars. After Mr. Davis gave her $27, she had $139. How much did she have initially?

2 The sum of two facing page numbers in a book is 145. What are the two page numbers?

3   Justin's age is $\frac{2}{5}$ of Julia's age. Julia is 27 years older than Justin. How old is Justin now?

4   The perimeter of an isosceles triangle is 32.7 inches. The length of its base is 9.5 inches. Find the length of each of the other two identical sides.

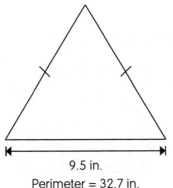

9.5 in.
Perimeter = 32.7 in.

5   Zoe was planning to bake some chocolate, strawberry, and raisin muffins for a large party. She was asked to bake half as many chocolate muffins as raisin muffins and three times as many strawberry muffins as chocolate muffins. She only had enough ingredients to bake 480 muffins. How many raisin muffins did she bake?

6   Mr. Smith rented a car for a day. The rental fee consists of a flat rate of $19.99 and $0.21 per additional mile. He paid $52.54 for the car rental. How many miles did Mr. Smith drive the car?

7 The sum of three consecutive positive numbers is 147. Find the product of the greatest and the smallest numbers.

8 Madison bought some blue and green pens and organized the information in a table.

Type of Pens	Number of Pens	Cost of One Pen
Blue	x	$0.80
Green	$\frac{1}{2}x + 3$	$0.60

She spent $10.60 altogether. How many blue pens did she buy?

9 A food manufacturer donates money to schools based on the number of its product labels that the school collects. The students at one school collected 2,100 product labels in three months. The number of labels collected in each of the first two months was three times the number of labels collected in the third month. How many product labels were collected in the third month?

10 The perimeter of triangle *ABC* is 33 inches. Find the length of the sides of the triangle.

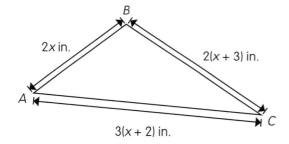

11 On a vacation to Paris, Anna's expenses on food, gifts, and accommodation was $80 less than three times her airfare. The total expenses for the trip was $2,660. How much was her airfare?

12 Megan cycles from home to school at a speed of 16 kilometers per hour. She cycles back on the same route at a speed of 15 kilometers per hour. The total time taken for the journey is $7\frac{3}{4}$ hours. Given that the distance from her house to school is d kilometers, write and solve an equation to find the total distance that Megan travels.

Chapter 3

Extra Practice and Homework
Algebraic Equations and Inequalities

Activity 4   Solving Algebraic Inequalities

Solve each inequality using addition and subtraction. Then, graph each solution set on a number line.

1   $27 + x < 10$

2   $9 \geq 12 - x$

3   $\frac{2}{5}x - \frac{5}{6} + \frac{3}{5}x < \frac{5}{12}$

4   $\frac{3}{4} \leq \frac{3}{4}x + \frac{7}{8} + \frac{1}{4}x$

5   $1.5x - 10 - 0.5x \leq 2$

6   $8 > 0.4x - 7 + 0.6x$

Solve each inequality using multiplication and division. Then, graph each solution set on a number line.

7 $6x > 6$

8 $3x \leq -2$

9 $-\frac{5}{2}x > 10$

10 $\frac{5}{6}x - \frac{1}{2} < \frac{1}{3}$

11 $12.3 - 0.7x < 6$

12 $3.3 \leq 0.75x - 0.45$

Solve each inequality using the four operations. Then, graph each solution set on a number line.

13 $8 + x < 10$

14 $11 \le 7 + 4x$

15 $0.1x - 7 < 11$

16 $7 \ge 2.4x + 9.4$

17 $3 < \frac{1}{7}x + 4$

18 $\frac{1}{6}x + \frac{1}{3} < 1$

Solve each inequality with parentheses using the four operations.

19 $3(y + 2) \le 18$

20 $6(2y - 1) > 3.6$

21 $2(9 - x) + x \le 16$

22 $5(4x - 5) \ge 3$

23 $\frac{1}{6}(a - 1) > \frac{1}{3}$

24 $-17 \le 5 - 2(3a - 1)$

25 $8 + 5(z - 4) < 13$

26 $-12 \ge 3(3z + 5)$

Extra Practice and Homework Course 2A

Extra Practice and Homework
Algebraic Equations and Inequalities

Activity 5   Real-World Problems: Algebraic Inequalities

Solve.

1 Noah's scores for four Spanish quizzes are 70, 75, 83, and 80. What score must he get on the next quiz to achieve an average of at least 80?

2 Mr. Miller is saving to buy a mountain bike that costs $245, excluding tax. He has already saved $28. What is the least amount of money Mr. Miller must save each week so that at the end of the 9th week, he has enough money to buy the bike? Round your answer to the nearest dollar.

3 When Samantha uses her calling card overseas, the cost of a phone call is $0.75 for the first three minutes and $0.12 for each additional minute, thereafter. Samantha plans to spend at most $3.60 to make a call. Find the greatest possible length of talk time. Round your answer to the nearest whole number.

4 A company is selling hot air balloon rides to raise money for a children's charity. The cost of going on a balloon ride is a flat rate of $50 and $15 per hour of flight time. Ms. Lopez plans to donate at most $85. Find the number of hours she can spend in the balloon ride. Round your answer to the nearest hour.

5   East High School's student council plans to buy some stools and chairs for a new student center. They need to buy 25 more chairs than stools. The chairs cost $32 each and the stools cost $28 each. The budget is $2,620. How many chairs can they buy?

6   The length of a rectangle is 3 inches longer than the width of the rectangle. The perimeter of the rectangle is at most 46 inches. Find the greatest possible length of the rectangle.

7   The sum of 3 times a number and 16 is more than 25. Write an inequality and solve it.

8   Ella is playing a computer game. She needs to score more than an average of 80 points for 4 games in order for her to win the game. She has scored 91 points, 75 points, and 77 points in her first three games. How many points must Ella score in her last game?

Name: _____ Date: _____

Mathematical Habit 3 Construct viable arguments

The sum of any two sides, $a + b$, of a triangle is greater than the third side, c. The triangle inequality test, $a + b > c$, can be used to test whether a given set of measurements of a triangle is valid. Explain whether a triangle with sides, $2x + 7$, $5 - 3x$, and 18 cm can be formed.

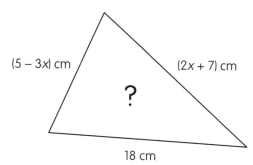

$(5 - 3x)$ cm $(2x + 7)$ cm

?

18 cm

1 **Mathematical Habit** **1** Persevere in solving problems

One integer is 15 more than $\frac{3}{4}$ of another integer. The sum of the integers is greater than 49. Find the least values for these two integers.

2 **Mathematical Habit** **6** Use precise mathematical language

The admission fees to a movie are as follows.

Category	Admission Fee
Adult	$8.50
Child	$5.50

On a certain Saturday, the number of adult tickets sold was $\frac{3}{4}$ of the number of child tickets sold. What was the greatest number of adult tickets sold if the box office receipts was at most $3,230?

© 2020 Marshall Cavendish Education Pte Ltd

Extra Practice and Homework Course 2A

Chapter

Extra Practice and Homework
Proportion and Percent of Change

Activity 1   Identifying Direct Proportion

Determine whether _y_ is directly proportional to _x_. If so, find the constant of proportionality. Then, write a direct proportion equation.

 ①

x	1	2	3
y	4	8	12

 ②

x	2	4	6
y	160	120	80

③

x	3	6	9
y	10	30	70

④

x	2	4	6
y	40	80	120

Determine whether each equation represents a direct proportion. If so, identify the constant of proportionality.

⑤ $\frac{1}{4}y = 5x$

⑥ $3y + 7 = x$

⑦ $a = 1.2b$

⑧ $2.5p = q - 1.6$

Solve.

9 The table shows the time, t hours, that a production line needs to make n calculators. Tell whether n is directly proportional to t. If so, give the constant of proportionality and tell what it represents in this situation. Then, write a direct proportion equation.

Number of Hours (t hours)	12	24	30
Number of Calculators (n)	30	60	75

10 The table shows the distance traveled by a car, d miles, after t hours. Tell whether d is directly proportional to t. If so, give the constant of proportionality and tell what it represents in this situation. Then, write a direct proportion equation.

Time (t hours)	1	2	3
Distance Traveled (d miles)	50	110	200

11 The admission fee to a museum is $8.50 per person. Given that the admission fee, *C* dollars, is directly proportional to the number of people, *n*, identify the constant of proportionality and write a direct proportion equation.

12 A baker requires 21 ounces of flour to make a large loaf of bread. Given that the amount of flour the baker needs, *w* ounces, is directly proportional to the number of loaves that he bakes, *n*, identify the constant of proportionality and write a direct proportion equation.

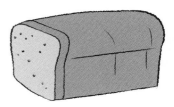

13 *a* is directly proportional to *b*, and *a* = 14 when *b* = 42. Write a direct proportion equation that relates *a* and *b*.

14 w is directly proportional to v, and $w = 6$ when $v = 10$. Write a direct proportion equation that relates w and v.

15 The amount Mr. Robinson earns is directly proportional to the number of hours he works. If Mr. Robinson earns $60.80 for 4 hours of work, find the constant of proportionality and write a direct proportion equation.

16 For every three minutes a faucet drips, one cup of water is wasted. The amount of water wasted is directly proportional to the amount of time the faucet drips. Find the constant of proportionality and write a direct proportion equation.

Chapter 4

Extra Practice and Homework
Proportion and Percent of Change

Activity 2   Representing Direct Proportion Graphically

State whether each graph represents a direct proportion. If so, find the constant of proportionality. Then, write a direct proportion equation.

1

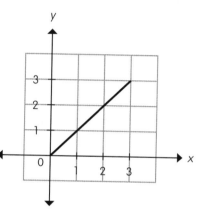

_____

2

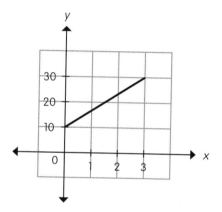

_____

3

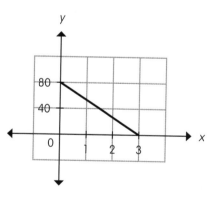

_____

4

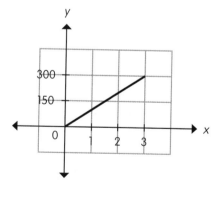

_____

Solve.

5 The amount of money Ms. Long earns is directly proportional to the number of hours she works. The graph shows the amount of money, w dollars, Ms. Long earns in t hours.

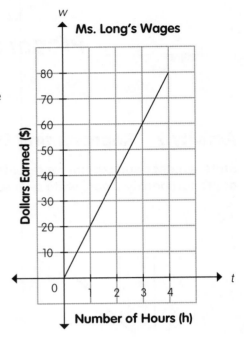

a Find the constant of proportionality. What does this value represent in this situation?

b How much does Ms. Long earn if she works 3 hours?

c How long does Ms. Long work if she earns $70?

6 The height of a seedling is directly proportional to the number of days since it was planted. The graph shows the height of the seedling, h centimeters, after x days.

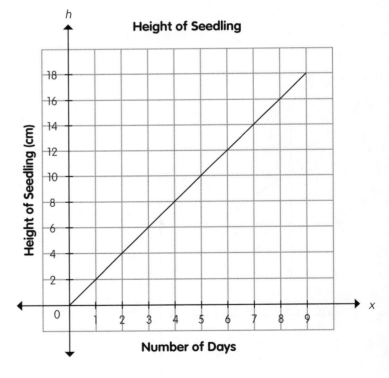

a Write the direct proportion equation.

b Explain what the point (5, 10) represents in this situation.

c What is the height of the seedling after 3 days? After one week?

d How many days will it take for the seedling to reach a height of at least 18 centimeters?

7 The amount of Japanese yen you get depends on the number of U.S. dollars you exchange. Graph the relationship between y Japanese yen and x U.S. dollars. Use 1 unit on the horizontal axis to represent 1 U.S. dollar and 1 unit on the vertical axis to represent 100 Japanese yen.

U.S. dollars (x)	0	2	4	6	8
Japanese yen (y)	0	200	400	600	800

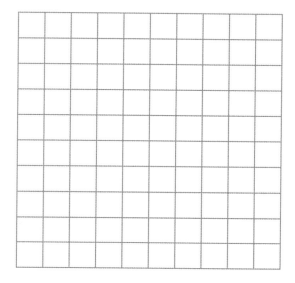

a Does the amount of Japanese yen vary directly with the number of U.S. dollars?

b What is the exchange rate when you convert U.S. dollars to Japanese yen?

c Write the direct proportion equation.

d Explain what the point (2, 200) represents in this situation.

e Ms. Allen exchanges 600 Japanese yen for U.S. dollars. What amount of money, in U.S. dollars, does she receive?

f Mr. Allen exchanges 7 U.S. dollars for Japanese yen. What amount of money, in Japanese yen, does he receive?

Chapter 4

Extra Practice and Homework
Proportion and Percent of Change

Activity 3   Real-World Problems: Direct Proportion

Write a direct variation equation and find each indicated value.

1   *a* varies directly as *b*, and $a = 4$ when $b = 24$.

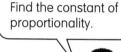

Find the constant of proportionality.

   a Write an equation that relates *a* and *b*.

   b Find *a* when $b = 63$.

   c Find *b* when $a = 7$.

2   *y* varies directly as *x*, and $y = 18$ when $x = \frac{1}{2}$.

   a Write an equation that relates *y* and *x*.

   b Find *x* when $y = 252$.

   c Find *y* when $x = \frac{1}{3}$.

In each table, p is directly proportional to q. Fill in each table.

3

p	20	40	
q	4		16

4

p	1	3	
q		27	90

Solve.

5 The cost of baseball caps, C dollars, is directly proportional to the number of baseball caps, n, purchased. Mackenzie purchased 12 baseball caps for $96.

   a Find the cost of a baseball cap.

   b Write an equation that relates C and n.

   c Find the value of C when $n = 20$.

6 The amount of money donated at a charity fundraising event, A, is directly proportional to the number of people, n, at the event. 6 people at the event donated a total of $120.

   a Find the amount donated by each person at the event.

   b Write an equation that relates the amount of money donated, A, and the number of people at the event, n.

   c How much did 50 people at the event donate?

7 Emma can type 275 words in 5 minutes. The number of words she types, w, is directly proportional to the length of time she takes to type, t minutes.

   a Find the constant of proportionality.

   b Write an equation that relates w and t.

   c How many minutes will it take her to type a 935-word document?

8 Blake needs to determine the height of each tree on his tree farm. He knows that the height of the tree, h feet, is directly proportional to the length of its shadow, d feet. The length of a shadow cast by an 8-foot tall tree is 5 feet.

   a Find the constant of proportionality.

   b Write an equation that relates the height, h, of the tree and the length of its shadow, d.

   c Use your equation to find the height of a tree that casts a shadow that is 12 feet long.

Use a proportion to solve each question.

9   4 cans of grapefruit juice cost $3.36. Find the cost of one dozen cans of grapefruit juice.

10 It costs $78 to rent a pair of skis for 3 days. Find the cost of renting the skis for a week.

11 Timothy rides his bike at an average speed of 14 miles per hour. How many miles will he ride in $2\frac{1}{2}$ hours?

12 To make fruit punch, Sofia mixes lemonade with orange juice in the ratio 5 : 9. She uses 40 ounces of lemonade. How many ounces of orange juice does she use?

13 John buys a pair of shoes for $52 and pays $2.60 sales tax. How much sales tax will his friend pay if his friend purchases a shirt for $28?

14 The cost of a piece of vacant land (a 'lot') in New York City, C dollars, is directly proportional to the area of the land, a square feet. A 2,000-square foot vacant lot costs $129,920. Find the cost for a 3,600-square foot vacant lot.

15 A company invests $50,000 in a savings account that pays 3% interest per year.

    a Write a direct proportion equation that relates interest, I, and years, t.

    b How much interest will the company earn in 2 years?

16 A machine can pack 60 packets of pasta in 5 minutes.

    a How long does it take the machine to pack 240 packets of pasta?

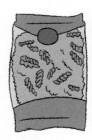

    b How many packets of pasta can the machine pack in an hour?

Chapter 4

Extra Practice and Homework
Proportion and Percent of Change

Activity 4   Identifying Inverse Proportion

Determine whether two quantities are in inverse proportion. If so, find the constant of proportionality.

x	100	50	10
y	2	4	20

x	6	4	2
y	20	40	80

x	3	6	9
y	10	20	30

4

x	2	6	10
y	210	70	42

Determine whether each equation represents an inverse proportion. If so, find the constant of proportionality.

5 $y = 15x$

6 $xy = \dfrac{1}{4}$

7 $20y = \dfrac{4}{x}$

8 $xy + 3 = 7$

Each graph represents an inverse proportion. Find the constant of proportionality.

9

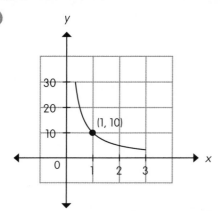

The constant of proportionality is _____.

10

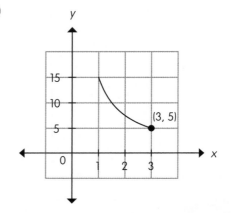

The constant of proportionality is _____.

11

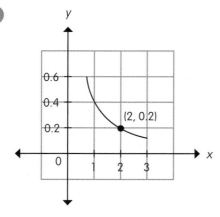

The constant of proportionality is _____.

12

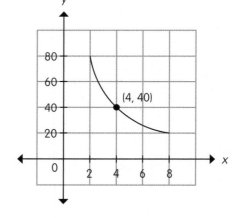

The constant of proportionality is _____.

Solve.

13 The density of a substance is the mass of the substance per unit of volume. The density of the element americium is inversely proportional to its volume. The graph shows the relationship between the density of americium, p grams per cubic centimeters, and its volume, v cubic centimeters.

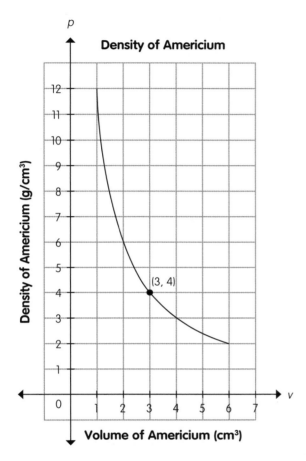

a Use the graph to determine the constant of proportionality. Then, write an inverse proportion equation.

b Explain what the constant of proportionality represents in this situation.

c Explain what the point (3, 4) represents in this situation.

14 A tank has a fixed capacity. The time it takes to fill the empty tank, *t* minutes, is inversely proportional to the rate of water flowing into the tank, *r* pints per minute. The graph shows the relationship between *r* and *t*.

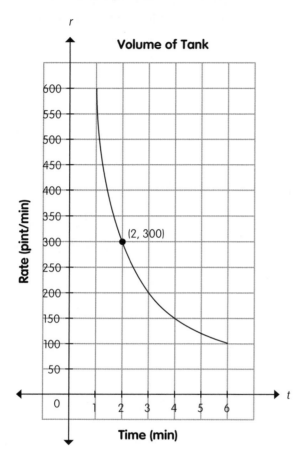

a Use the graph to determine the constant of proportionality. Then, write an inverse proportion equation.

b Explain what the point (2, 300) represents in this situation.

c How much time will it take to fill the empty tank if the water is flowing at a rate of 150 pints per minute?

15 s is inversely proportional to t, and $s = 12$ when $t = 7$.

a Find the constant of proportionality.

b Write an inverse equation relating s and t.

c Find the value of s when $t = 5$.

16 y is inversely proportional to x, and $y = 6$ when $x = 7.5$.

a Write an inverse equation relating x and y.

b Find the value of y when $x = 2$.

17 The length of time, y hours, it takes to put a jigsaw puzzle together is inversely proportional to the number of children, x, working on it. It takes 6 hours for 16 children to put the jigsaw puzzle together. How many children are needed to put the same jigsaw puzzle together in 4 hours?

18 The number of hours, y, it takes to drive from town P to town Q is inversely proportional to the average speed of a car, x miles per hour. It takes Jeremiah $3\frac{1}{2}$ hours to drive from Town P to Town Q at an average speed of 60 miles per hour on a particular day. How long will it take Jeremiah to travel from Town P to Town Q if his average driving speed is 70 miles per hour instead?

Chapter 4

Extra Practice and Homework
Proportion and Percent of Change

Activity 5   Percent Increase and Decrease

Solve.

1 A vine, which was 2 feet high, grew 18% over two weeks. How high was the vine after two weeks?

2 A 55-gallon barrel was filled to the brim and was left out in the open. 12% of the water was lost after three days of evaporation. Find the volume of water in the barrel after three days.

3 The cost price of a box of cereal is $1.80. The markup for each box of cereal is 60%. Find the selling price of each box of cereal.

4 The shirts available in a clothing store are of sizes S, M and L. A total of 240 shirts are sold in a day. 20% of the shirts are of size S and 45% are of size M. Find the number of shirts sold for each of the sizes.

5   The height of a plant was 2.5 feet. After 2 weeks, it grew to 4 feet. After 4 weeks, it grew to 5.5 feet. What is the percentage increase in its height at 4 weeks compared with

a   its initial height?

b   its height at 2 weeks?

6 Last year, there were 48 members in a chess club. This year, there are 55 members in the club. Find the percent increase in the number of members in the club. Round your answer to the nearest whole number.

7 At a store, the price of a box of chocolates is $12.50. During a sale, the price of the chocolates is $11. Find the percent of discount during the sale.

8 The original price of a tablet sold in an electronics store was $308. Members of the electronics store can purchase the tablet at a lower price of $246.40. Use proportion to find the percent of discount for members.

Chapter 4

Extra Practice and Homework
Proportion and Percent of Change

Activity 6   Real-World Problems: Percent Increase and Decrease

Solve.

1 Mr. Ruiz bought a truck for $2,700. He sold it at a profit of 20% to Ms. Jackson. Ms. Jackson also sold it but at a loss of 15%.

a How much did Mr. Ruiz sell the truck for?

b How much did Ms. Jackson sell the truck for?

2 Mr. Patel's new company manufactures cell phones. The company produced 1,200 phones for the first month. He now expects that the number of cell phones produced to increase by 15% each month. Find the number of cell phones he expects his company to produce in

a the second month,

b the third month.

3 The tax on a pair of shoes is $3.90. The tax levied is 5%.

   a Find the price of shoes before tax.

   b The pair of shoes is sold at a profit of 10%. Find the selling price of the pair of shoes after tax.

4 200 students were surveyed and were asked to choose their favorite primary color. 35% of the students chose yellow, 20% of the remaining students chose red and the rest chose blue. How many more students chose blue than red?

5 At a fruit store, 68% of the fruit sold are oranges and the rest are nectarines and apples. The number of nectarines is $\frac{3}{5}$ of the number of apples. There are 400 pieces of fruit in all. How many nectarines are there?

6 Ms. Harris had some money. She spent 28% of her money on bills and spent $\frac{4}{9}$ of the remaining amount on a dress. She then had $192 left.

a Find the cost of the dress.

b Find the amount Ms. Harris had at first.

Name: _____ Date: _____

Mathematical Habit 3 Construct viable arguments

Juan was given information on a piece of metal that was made up of an alloy of copper, zinc, and lead. It contained $\frac{3}{5}$ copper and 37% zinc by mass. The difference in the masses of zinc and copper was 9.2 pounds. He had to find the mass of lead in the metal.

Check if Juan did the right calculations. If not, give an explanation and show the correct calculations.

Juan's workings:

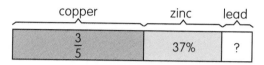

$\frac{3}{5} \times 37 = 22.2\%$

22.2% of 9.2 lb $= \frac{222}{1000} \times 9.2$

$= 2.04$ pounds (correct to 2 decimal places)

There was 2.04 pounds of lead in the piece of metal.

1 **Mathematical Habit** **4** Use mathematical models

The resistance, R, of a piece of wire is directly proportional to the length of the wire, ℓ, and inversely proportional to the cross-sectional area of the wire, A.

a Write an equation to represent the relationship. Use k for the constant of proportionality.

b Explain the effect on the resistance if the length of a piece of wire is doubled.

2 **Mathematical Habit** **4** Use mathematical models

The length of time it takes to tile a locker room floor, t hours, varies directly with the number of tiles needed, n, and varies inversely with the number of people laying the tiles, p.

a Write an equation to represent the relationship. Use k for the constant of variation.

b It takes 21 hours for 4 people to lay 1,500 tiles. Use your equation in **a** to determine how long it will take 6 people to lay 5,000 tiles. Round your answer to the nearest whole hour.